Life is Sweet, Y'all

Given to:

From:

Date:

My word of wit & wisdom:

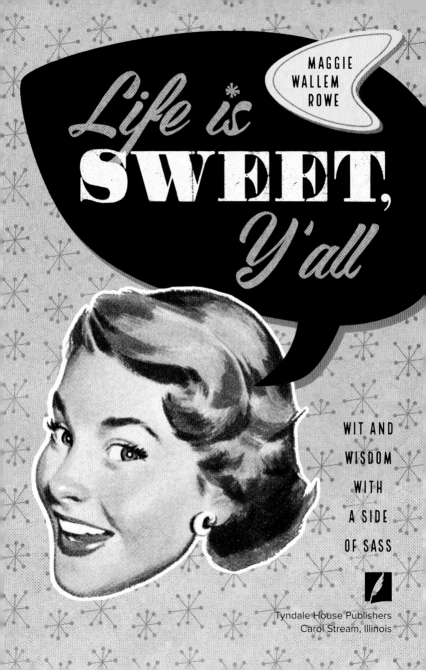

MAGGIE
WALLEM
ROWE

Life is
SWEET,
Y'all

WIT AND
WISDOM
WITH
A SIDE
OF SASS

Tyndale House Publishers
Carol Stream, Illinois

LIVING
EXPRESSIONS
COLLECTION

Living Expressions invites you to explore
God's Word in a way that is refreshing to
your spirit and restorative to your soul.

Visit Tyndale online at tyndale.com.

Tyndale, Tyndale's quill logo, *Living Expressions*, and the Living Expressions logo are
registered trademarks of Tyndale House Ministries.

Life Is Sweet, Y'all: Wit and Wisdom with a Side of Sass

Designed by Julie Chen

Unless otherwise indicated, all Scripture quotations are taken from the *Holy Bible*, New
Living Translation, copyright © 1996, 2004, 2015 by Tyndale House Foundation; used by
permission of Tyndale House Publishers, Carol Stream, Illinois 60188; all rights reserved.
Scripture quotations marked ESV are from The ESV® Bible (The Holy Bible, English
Standard Version®), copyright © 2001 by Crossway, a publishing ministry of Good News
Publishers; used by permission; all rights reserved. Scripture quotation marked MSG is
taken from *The Message*, copyright © 1993, 2002, 2018 by Eugene H. Peterson; used
by permission of NavPress; all rights reserved; represented by Tyndale House Publishers.
Scripture quotation marked NIV is taken from the Holy Bible, *New International Version*,®
NIV®; copyright © 1973, 1978, 1984, 2011 by Biblica, Inc.®; used by permission; all rights
reserved worldwide.

For information about special discounts for bulk purchases, please contact Tyndale House
Publishers at csresponse@tyndale.com, or call 1-855-277-9400.

ISBN 978-1-4964-5313-6

Printed in China

28	27	26	25	24	23	22
7	6	5	4	3	2	1

To my grandchildren

Wisdom

is sweet to

your soul.

PROVERBS 24:14

CONTENTS

1. F Is for Family 1
2. Fancy Seeing You Here! 2
3. Zip That Lip! 8
4. "Because I Said So" 10
5. Don't Be a Worrywart! 11
6. Make Yourself Useful 16
7. Hope's Not Wishful Thinking, Darlin' 18
8. Raising Sprouts 19
9. That One Who's Done You Wrong 24
10. Keep Your Word 26
11. What You Plant You're Gonna Pick 27
12. Your Own Kind of Beautiful 32
13. Put Down That Party Line 34
14. Eyes Straight Ahead, Missy! 35
15. Don't Have Faith—Do It! 40
16. Is There Any Justice in This World? 42
17. Pray for Me, Y'all! 43
18. Take a Rest 48
19. If You've Got a Rooster . . . 50
20. Humble and Kind 51
21. Peace, Child . . . Peace 56
22. Jump off the Bandwagon 58
23. When Life Puts the Squeeze on You 59
24. Have FOMO? 64
25. Keep an Extinguisher Handy 66
26. Like a Hammock between Cornstalks 67

27. Love Them Anyway 72
28. Don't Put It Off 74
29. I've Got the Joy 75
30. Honest to Goodness 80
31. R-E-S-P-E-C-T 82
32. Live Soul Strong 83
33. Pretty Is as Pretty Does 88
34. Just Wait till I Tell Your Father 90
35. The Beauty of Community 91
36. God Will Provide 96
37. Patience, Sweet Pea . . . Patience 98
38. You're the Genuine Article 99
39. For the Love of God 104
40. Everyone Can Help Someone 106
41. On the One Hand . . . 107
42. Attitude Is a Choice 112
43. God with Us 114
44. You Can Do It! 115
45. Say You're Sorry 120
46. Holier than Thou? 122
47. A Heart as Soft as Butter 123
48. Security and Exchange 126
49. Confidence Looks Good on You, Girl! 127
50. The Best Way to Have a Friend 130
51. Goodness Gracious! 134
52. Outlive Your Life 138

RECIPES

Just like Mom Used to Make

1. Ozark Apple Pudding 6

2. Pearl Jean's Peanut Butter Fudge 14

3. Gimme-Some-Sugar Cookies 22

4. Sassy Pecan Tassies 30

5. Cheddar Coins 38

6. Pimiento Cheese Spread 46

7. Nana's BaNana Bread 54

8. Shirley's Chocolate Zucchini Bread 62

9. Honey-Let-Me-Tell-Ya Cake 70

10. Miss Eunice's Hot-Fudge-in-a-Jar 78

11. If-Life-Gives-You-Lemons Pie 86

12. Sweetie-Potato Pie 94

13. Sunday Fried Chicken 102

14. Country Bean Salad 110

15. Sweetly Southern Tea 118

God put me on earth to accomplish a number of things. Right now I'm so far behind I should live forever.*

* Bill Watterson, *Calvin & Hobbes*

x

F Is for Family

You know the old saying about family: You can't live with 'em, and you can't live without 'em. We all have a few loose branches on our family tree along with an impressive collection of nuts. Maybe you have kids who are like a matched set of dueling pistols, or you've got a brother-in-law who can't weigh facts because he's got a scale full of opinions already. But as ornery and cantankerous as family members can be, they're yours. If the most important commandments in Scripture are to love God and your neighbor, it's good to remember that your neighbor is as near as the man or woman, boy or girl who happens to be under your roof. And if someday your family tree branches off in different directions? You still share the same deep roots.

Submit to one another out of reverence for Christ.
EPHESIANS 5:21

I sustain myself with the love of family.
Maya Angelou

Fancy Seeing You Here!

❋

It's said that success is being able to tell the truth at your high school reunion. Don't we sometimes wish we could show those who never thought we'd amount to anything that we've made something special of our lives after all? The problem comes with defining one slippery little seven-letter word: *success*. Is success landing a dream job that impresses others? Is it having plenty of money in the bank, a happy marriage, and obedient children? Those are wonderful blessings, but factors that depend on the actions of other people or the world's standards are unreliable rulers for measuring success. Instead, ask yourself whether you are doing the best you can and living in a way that demonstrates honor and integrity before God and people. If your answer is yes, it sure sounds like success to me!

Work willingly at whatever you do, as though you were working for the Lord rather than for people.

COLOSSIANS 3:23

Somewhere along the way I learned an old folk saying. . . . If you want to succeed in life, the saying goes, you must pick three bones to carry with you at all times: a wishbone, a backbone, and a funny bone.

Reba McEntire, Comfort from a Country Quilt

If you want to frost

a cake like a pro,

use a fresh

paint-stirring

stick.

Easy peasy!

TIP

Learn your lesson the first time. There's no education in the second kick of a mule.

OZARK APPLE PUDDING

First Lady Bess Truman served a version of this dessert at the White House when her husband, Harry S. Truman, was president. Both of them were from Missouri, a state where part of the Ozarks region is found. Top the pudding with whipped cream or vanilla ice cream at your house!

✳ INGREDIENTS

2 eggs
1½ cups granulated sugar
⅔ cup all-purpose flour
2 teaspoons baking powder

¼ teaspoon salt
1 cup chopped apple
1 cup chopped walnuts
1 teaspoon vanilla extract

 # INSTRUCTIONS

1. Preheat oven to 350 degrees. Grease and flour a 9-inch square pan.

2. In a medium-sized bowl, beat the eggs with a mixer and slowly add the sugar, beating until light and creamy.

3. Combine the flour, baking powder, and salt in a small bowl; add to egg mixture, blending well.

4. Fold chopped apple and walnuts into batter; add vanilla.

5. Pour batter into greased and floured pan and bake 30 minutes.

Zip That Lip!

Life's full of problems, usually more than you can say grace over. No wonder you get frustrated at times! Maybe you feel like snatchin' someone bald-headed or pitching a plate at the wall, but venting your anger will make more of a mess than you're already in. Step back, sit down, and take a deep breath. Several of them, in fact. How much of this situation is yours to fix? If a good remedy comes to mind, use it. But if other people are responsible, let them take the consequences, even if they're not willing to take the blame. If they won't listen to you, at least you'll know you've done what you could. Hold your peace and entrust the situation to the One in charge of the world. Thankfully, that's not you!

Understand this, my dear brothers and sisters: You must all be quick to listen, slow to speak, and slow to get angry.
JAMES 1:19

A dryer sheet
tucked in your
luggage between
trips will keep
your bags fresh.

TIP

"Because I Said So"

What parent hasn't used the words "Because I said so" in a moment of exasperation? When we're young, with little experience in the world, our parents can't always explain everything to our satisfaction. But when it comes to questioning authority figures or complicated situations as adults, "Because I said so" just isn't good enough. With so much misinformation out there, how do you know which voices to trust? It's important to check the source and compare the information you read with what's being reported elsewhere. You also want to make sure something you've heard has not been taken out of context. God's Word is faithful, reliable, and true—but when it comes to man's information, make sure to measure it at least twice before you share it once!

Jesus told him, "I am the way, the truth, and the life."
JOHN 14:6

If you ever challenge someone to a battle of wits, make sure you're well armed.
Maggie Wallem Rowe

Don't Be a Worrywart!

Are you fretting about something before it even gets here? That's like spoilin' Saturday night by counting the hours to Monday morning. Worry is always trying to win a war in our heads. It's a bully who spends our peace of mind like pocket change. But you can kick the bully out of your brain and your business. Your heavenly Father says to commit your troubles to him, no matter how big they might be, and to listen for his voice telling you which way to turn. It takes a load off your shoulders when you know God's watching out for you. He cares for your life and your loved ones even more than you do.

Don't worry about anything; instead, pray about everything. Tell God what you need, and thank him for all he has done.
PHILIPPIANS 4:6

Worry is like a rocking chair. It gives you something to do, but it doesn't get you anywhere.
Erma Bombeck

Use it up.
Wear it out.
Make it do,
or do without.*

* World War II slogan

PEARL JEAN'S PEANUT BUTTER FUDGE

A heritage recipe from a Kentucky-born mama whose descendants were persuaded to part with it!

✳ INGREDIENTS

4 cups granulated sugar

4 tablespoons unsweetened baking cocoa

4 tablespoons light corn syrup

2 cups whole milk

4 tablespoons butter, divided

½ cup creamy peanut butter

2 teaspoons vanilla extract

Candy thermometer

✳ INSTRUCTIONS

1. Generously butter a 9 x 13 pan and set aside.

2. Combine sugar, cocoa, corn syrup, and milk in a heavy-bottomed saucepan. Heat on medium-high, stirring constantly with a wooden spoon.

3. When mixture starts to boil, add 2 tablespoons of butter.

4. Continue stirring and cooking until the candy thermometer reaches 234 degrees.

5. Remove from heat and cool to 110 degrees. Add remaining butter (2 tablespoons), peanut butter, and vanilla.

6. Place saucepan in cold sink water and stir mixture until it starts to thicken and lose its sheen. Pour into prepared 9 x 13 pan and refrigerate until firm. Cut into squares and store at room temperature in airtight containers, or layer fudge between sheets of wax paper and freeze.

Make Yourself Useful

Did you know there are employers out there whose only on-the-job training consists of telling their workers to get busy and make themselves useful? Now it's true that some folks are so lazy that all they wait for is sundown and payday, but most of us would rather put physical and mental muscle into making a positive difference in this world. From the beginning of creation, God designed us to be fruitful and to meet one another's needs through loving acts of service. It's in our very nature to feel deep satisfaction when our efforts truly help others. Someone once advised that we should not feel bad when people seem to remember us only when they need us. Instead, we should consider it a privilege that we're like candles that help light the path when there is darkness. Shine on!

Always work enthusiastically for the Lord, for you know that nothing you do for the Lord is ever useless.
1 CORINTHIANS 15:58

I did my best, and God did the rest.
Hattie McDaniel

For evenly sliced
strawberries,
use an egg slicer.
But first, hull the
berry by pushing
a straw through the
middle, working
from the bottom up.

Hope's Not Wishful Thinking, Darlin'

Most of us remember making a wish as kids before we blew out the candles on our birthday cakes, or looking at the night sky and wishing on the brightest star. Wishful thinking is *wistful* thinking, a vague idea that someday you'll get what you're hankering after. But true hope . . . now that's another thing altogether. Hebrews 6:19 says that when we place our hope in Christ, we have something solid and substantial—an anchor for our souls—and the verse below tells us that those who hope in the Lord will find new strength and soar on wings like eagles. Remember, though, that soaring starts with a single step of faith. Before you know it, you'll be running. And then . . . look out, world—you're gonna fly!

Those who trust in the Lord will find new strength.
They will soar high on wings like eagles. They will
run and not grow weary. They will walk and not faint.
ISAIAH 40:31

Hope may not be your mother tongue,
but it's a language you can learn.
Maggie Wallem Rowe

Raising Sprouts

Got any children at home or grandkids you're helping to raise? Perhaps you're a Sunday school teacher or childcare worker. You're busier than a moth in a mitten and as tired as a mule that slogged a mile in the mud. And you wonder sometimes whether those young'uns will turn out all right because, Lord help you, it sure is hard to tell most days! That's when it's good to remember that God's not done with them yet. Think of the kids as time-release seeds. You're working the earth of their hearts by sowing strong character that will lead to a future harvest you can't see just yet. Have faith that God loves them more than you do and remember that they are never out of his sight.

My Spirit will not leave them, and neither will these words I have given you. They will be on your lips and on the lips of your children and your children's children forever.
ISAIAH 59:21

Have a heart that never hardens, and a temper that never tires, and a touch that never hurts.
Miss Jenny in Charles Dickens's Our Mutual Friend

Always be on time. Otherwise you're being disrespectful of other folks' time.

GIMME-SOME-SUGAR COOKIES

When Southern grand-mas ask for "sugar," they're expecting a kiss, but the grandkids will be asking for these cookies instead!

✳ INGREDIENTS

1 cup butter
1 cup vegetable or canola oil
1 cup granulated sugar
1 cup powdered sugar
2 eggs
1 teaspoon vanilla extract

4 cups all-purpose flour
1 teaspoon baking soda
1 teaspoon salt
1 teaspoon cream of tartar
Sparkling sugar

✳ INSTRUCTIONS

1. Preheat oven to 375 degrees.

2. In a large bowl, cream butter, oil, granulated sugar and powdered sugar, eggs, and vanilla.

3. In a medium-sized bowl, combine flour, baking soda, salt, and cream of tartar. Mix well.

4. Add the flour mixture to the creamed mixture and mix thoroughly. Chill in fridge for 1 hour.

5. Shape dough from rounded teaspoonfuls into balls and place on ungreased cookie sheets. Press dough balls down slightly with the tines of a fork and sprinkle with sparkling sugar. Bake at 375 degrees for 10–12 minutes or until edges are golden brown. Cool for 2 minutes before placing on wire racks. Makes 5 dozen. *Sweet!*

That One Who's Done You Wrong

✳

Yep, you know the one. It's the man whose name was once as sweet as honey on your tongue but now burns your lips. Or maybe it's the woman who acted like she was your best friend until it became as clear as a freshly washed window that she wasn't. Few things on this side of eternity are as hard to stomach as betrayal. Only someone we've loved deeply has the power to hurt us that badly. You can't change how he cheated on you, or how she failed you when you needed her, but here's what you can do: Rise up. Rise above the betrayal by refusing to let the one who hurt you bring you down. Rise up by rejecting retaliation. Rise up by remembering that God sees what others don't, and he will never, ever leave you. Rise up!

Don't repay evil for evil. Don't retaliate with insults when people insult you. Instead, pay them back with a blessing. That is what God has called you to do, and he will grant you his blessing.
1 PETER 3:9

A wet cotton ball
works well to pick
up small broken
glass shards you
can't see easily.

TIP

Keep Your Word

Have you ever had a come-to-Jesus meeting with someone because they made promises they rarely kept? It sure is wonderful when you can trust the people you live and work with. You know how important it is that you can rely on them, but they need to be able to set store by you too. Trust is like a bank account. If you put in regular deposits of promises fulfilled, there'll be enough to get you through an unfortunate withdrawal or two. Say what you mean and mean what you say. Then no matter what you might lose, you'll have kept your integrity. Don't let your mouth write checks that your friends and family can't take to the bank. Keep your word!

To the faithful you show yourself faithful;
to those with integrity you show integrity.
PSALM 18:25

A person who promises a gift but doesn't give it
is like clouds and wind that bring no rain.
PROVERBS 25:14

What You Plant You're Gonna Pick

Every farmer expects that what goes into the ground is what's gonna come out of it. We reap what we sow. If you're happy with the past choices you've made, you can usually anticipate good results. But as human beings, we're gonna mess up at times, just like our first parents did in the Garden of Eden. God gave them everything they needed, but they went looking for more. We're all gonna make mistakes in this lifetime—lots of them. But the good news of the gospel is that God's forgiveness flows as freely as water poured from a pitcher. When we admit we've done wrong, God is faithful and just to forgive us and make us as clean as a white shirt boiled with lemons!

Everyone has sinned; we all fall short of
God's glorious standard. Yet God, in his grace,
freely makes us right in his sight.

ROMANS 3:23-24

Gossip is like kudzu—it keeps on spreading.

SASSY PECAN TASSIES

The recipe for these little
tarts is more than a century
old. Taste one and you'll know
why it's considered a classic.

✳ INGREDIENTS

½ cup butter, softened
3 ounces cream cheese,
  softened
1 cup all-purpose flour

¾ cup packed light brown sugar
1 egg
1 teaspoon vanilla extract
¾ cup finely chopped pecans

✳ INSTRUCTIONS

1. Preheat oven to 325 degrees. Grease 24 miniature muffin wells.

2. In a small bowl, combine butter and cream cheese with a beater, mixing until well blended.

3. Add flour and mix well with beater. Cover and chill dough in refrigerator one hour or until firm.

4. In a separate small bowl, combine brown sugar, egg, and vanilla; mix well. Stir in nuts.

5. Shape chilled dough into 24 balls and press into greased minia-ture muffin wells. Top each ball of dough with pecan mixture until the muffin well is ¾ full.

6. Bake at 325 degrees for 25 minutes or until the edges are light brown.

7. Cool 5 minutes; then remove tarts from muffin wells. If the tassies don't disappear immediately, store leftovers in an airtight con-tainer. They also freeze well when layered between wax paper.

Your Own Kind of Beautiful

※

When you were little, did you ever dream of growing up to look like your favorite doll? Maybe you coveted curls like Shirley Temple's or a curvy figure like Barbie's. A small boy might have wanted a brawny physique like G.I. JOE's. It's easy for children to feel "less than" when they compare themselves to idealized playthings, and the same is true of us when we compare ourselves to the airbrushed versions of celebrities our culture promotes. We've all heard that beauty is in the eye of the beholder, but do we realize that's actually true? God made us and pronounced us good. He sees us as uniquely and wonderfully made, precious beyond price in his sight. Human love is biased and subjective, but God's love sees us as we truly are. You are your own kind of beautiful, and nobody else can compare to that.

Don't be concerned about the outward beauty of fancy hairstyles, expensive jewelry, or beautiful clothes.
You should clothe yourselves instead with the beauty that comes from within, the unfading beauty of a gentle and quiet spirit, which is so precious to God.
1 PETER 3:3-4

Out of buttermilk
for making your
pancakes or
cornbread?
Combine one
tablespoon of
vinegar with a
cup of whole milk.

TIP

Put Down That Party Line

✳

When telephone service was new to the United States, many rural households were on party lines. You couldn't have a private conversation with your mama in Minnesota without the risk of nosy neighbors listening in. Party lines on phones have disappeared, but they've been replaced by social media, where all kinds of tattling goes on under the guise of news or even "prayer requests." Just because something juicy is posted publicly doesn't mean it's not plain old gossip. We can't always keep our names out of other people's mouths, but we sure as shootin' can hush our own when we're tempted to pass on stories that aren't ours to tell. When it comes to sharing sensitive information about another person, if in doubt, leave it out!

A gossip goes around telling secrets,
so don't hang around with chatterers.
PROVERBS 20:19

Eyes Straight Ahead, Missy!

Students with a propensity to let their eyes wander during examinations are sometimes reprimanded by their teachers with the stern warning, "Eyes straight ahead!" As we age, we may still have a tendency to look around and stare at others' lives rather than focus on the direction of our own. We know where we've been, but we can't tell diddly-squat about where we're headed. The future can look like a fearful place sometimes, full of unknowns. But here's the good news: We have a powerful Creator who can be fully known, and he's got your future in his loving hands. Life's got to be lived forward, not backward. The next time you start worrying about what's to come, remember how God has directed you in the past. With your eyes firmly fixed on him in faith, simply do the next thing you know to do, and leave the outcome to him.

No eye has seen, no ear has heard, and no mind has imagined what God has prepared for those who love him.
1 CORINTHIANS 2:9

Seek to be the kind
of friend you'd love
to have yourself.

CHEDDAR COINS

If you're partial to the cheese straws so popular in the South, you'll love these!

✳ INGREDIENTS

½ cup butter, softened
1½ cups all-purpose flour
½ teaspoon baking powder
½ teaspoon salt

3 cups shredded sharp
  cheddar cheese
¼ teaspoon cayenne pepper

✳ INSTRUCTIONS

1. Preheat oven to 400 degrees.

2. Mix all the ingredients in a large mixing bowl till thoroughly blended.

3. Flour your hands lightly and pat a heaping tablespoon of dough into a small circle about ¼ of an inch thick.

4. Place circles on two large ungreased baking sheets about an inch apart. Bake 12–14 minutes, until just starting to brown.

5. Cool on wire rack. Store any leftovers in an airtight container or freeze for your next guests!

Don't Have Faith—Do It!

Has anyone tried to encourage you by telling you to "just have faith" that everything will work out? They mean well, but those words can be as empty as a bird's nest in December. When you're worried about something or someone, positive thinking doesn't always cut it. Scripture tells us that real faith comes from hearing about Christ and letting that good news point the way toward hope in every situation. It also tells us to act on what we have heard and know about Christ. When you face a difficult situation, ask God to show you the next steps to take. Instead of *having* faith, let's do it instead!

Don't fool yourself into thinking that you are a listener when you are anything but, letting the Word go in one ear and out the other. *Act* on what you hear!
JAMES 1:22-23, MSG

Faith never knows where it is being led, but it loves and knows the One Who is leading.
Oswald Chambers, My Utmost for His Highest

Want to make glass shower doors sparkle? Combine equal amounts of water and distilled white vinegar in a spray bottle; then spray the liquid on the doors. Wet a microfiber cloth, sprinkle on baking soda, and generously smear it on the glass. Let the mixture sit for a few minutes, then respray until the glass is lightly saturated. Five minutes later, wipe down with a soft scrubber.

TIP

Is There Any Justice in This World?

Some folks say that when it comes to wrongdoing, we want mercy for ourselves and justice for everyone else. But when it comes right down to it, something deep in our souls longs for a just world where rights are protected and wrongs are punished. It's easy to become cynical when we see injustice all around us. We're never promised we'll always be treated fairly, but we can do our level best to make sure others are. It's not enough just to know what's right; we need to *do* what's right as well. Keeping quiet about injustice never helps the victim, only the victimizer. Resolve to act on what you hear, and when you see something that's wrong, say something!

Learn to do good. Seek justice. Help the oppressed. Defend the cause of orphans. Fight for the rights of widows.
ISAIAH 1:17

It's a matter of taking the side of the weak against the strong, something the best people have always done.
Harriet Beecher Stowe

Pray for Me, Y'all!

Maybe you've heard the story about the little boy who was so disruptive in church one Sunday that his exasperated father finally picked him up and headed toward the back of the sanctuary. The congregation erupted in laughter when the boy called out over his daddy's shoulder, "Pray for me, y'all!" We can relate because there's a child of God in each of us who knows that in our sinful condition we desperately need help from on high. Ever wonder if prayer actually works? Whether or not we receive the answers we hope for, we can rest easy knowing that our prayers and petitions make an eternal difference. Why? Because Jesus told us to pray, and if anyone oughta know that prayer works, it's Jesus!

Everyone who asks, receives. Everyone who seeks, finds. And to everyone who knocks, the door will be opened.
MATTHEW 7:8

Prayer is the portal that brings the power of heaven down to earth. It is kryptonite to the enemy and to all his ploys against you.
Priscilla Shirer, Fervent

It's bad enough
when you misplace your
keys or cell phone, but what
really dills your pickle is not
remembering what to
do with them when
you find them.

PIMIENTO CHEESE SPREAD

You won't find many church potlucks in the South without pimiento cheese spread. It's dandy on crackers, in grilled cheese sandwiches, or even for topping burgers.

✳ INGREDIENTS

4 ounces cream cheese, softened

4 ounces (1 small jar) diced pimientos, drained

⅛ cup mayonnaise

1½ tablespoons onion, finely chopped

8 ounces shredded sharp cheddar cheese (about 3 cups)

 INSTRUCTIONS

1. In a large bowl, combine cream cheese, pimientos, mayonnaise, and onion with mixer until well blended.

2. Stir in cheddar cheese.

3. Refrigerate at least two hours before serving with crackers. Double the recipe for a crowd.

Take a Rest

Some of us fill our days so full that we wouldn't be able to catch our breath if it didn't come naturally! Sound like your life? Between your family, your work, and all your other responsibilities, maybe rest seems like a luxury you just can't afford. But here's the thing: We weren't created to live plumb tuckered out all the time. To stay healthy in mind and body, we need rest, and we need recreation. Think about that last word in a different way: *re-creation*. It means being made again. When we set aside our to-do lists, our souls can catch up with all the places our bodies have been. God rested on the seventh day; do you think that's more than a hint that we should too?

 In six days the LORD made heaven and earth, but on the seventh day he stopped working and was refreshed.
EXODUS 31:17

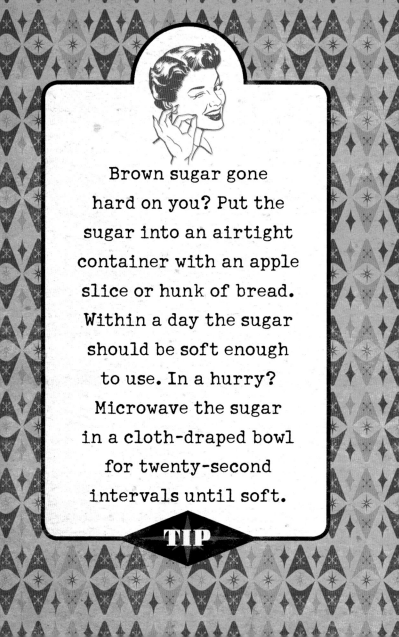

Brown sugar gone hard on you? Put the sugar into an airtight container with an apple slice or hunk of bread. Within a day the sugar should be soft enough to use. In a hurry? Microwave the sugar in a cloth-draped bowl for twenty-second intervals until soft.

TIP

If You've Got a Rooster . . .

Could be you've got some problems you've been trying to ignore, hoping they'll go away. Maybe it's the bills that keep coming when you've got too much month left and not enough money. Maybe it's the suspicion that someone you love is not being totally honest with you. Or maybe you're just not feeling up to par but keep putting off that doctor appointment. It's natural to want to focus on what's working in life and hope the rest will fix itself somehow. Yet sooner or later you will need to face your situation square on. Country folk know that if you've got a rooster, it's gonna crow. Decide to take one simple step today to schedule that doctor visit, have that difficult conversation with your loved one, or arrange a payment plan for those bills. You're not alone. God cares deeply about whatever's worrisome in your life. He's got this, friend.

Surely your goodness and unfailing love will pursue me all the days of my life, and I will live in the house of the LORD forever.

PSALM 23:6

Humble and Kind

Who doesn't want to be around someone who is consistently humble and kind? Maybe some folks you know are so full of themselves that you'd like to buy 'em for what they're worth and sell 'em for what they *think* they're worth. An inflated ego isn't attractive to anyone except the person who has it. Humility, on the other hand, is a beautiful quality. Humility is not weakness or meekness. It's not thinking less of yourself but thinking of yourself less. And being kind is not so much about random acts as it is about regular actions that become habit-forming, about looking at the world through eyes of mercy. It's treating others the way God treats us. If we strive each day to be humble and kind, we'll make a big difference in our small corners of the world.

Humble yourselves before the Lord,
and he will lift you up in honor.
JAMES 4:10

One kind word can warm three winter months.
Japanese proverb

A man convinced
against his will is of
the same opinion still.

NANA'S BANANA BREAD

Just like your granny used
to make . . . only maybe
better. This bread freezes beautifully,
so you can always have extra on hand for a friend.

✱ INGREDIENTS

4 ripe bananas, mashed
1 cup granulated sugar
½ cup butter, softened
   Pinch of salt
1 teaspoon baking powder
1 teaspoon baking soda
   (dissolve in a teaspoon or
   two of water)

2 eggs, beaten
2 cups all-purpose flour
   Pinches of cinnamon, brown
   sugar, and dry oatmeal

 **INSTRUCTIONS**

1. Preheat oven to 350 degrees. Grease four mini loaf pans.

2. In a large bowl, combine bananas, sugar, and butter with a mixer; then let stand for 15 minutes.

3. Add salt, baking powder, baking soda, eggs, and flour. Mix until combined.

4. Pour into mini loaf pans, filling ⅔ full. Sprinkle a little cinnamon, brown sugar, and dry oatmeal on top of the batter in each pan.

5. Bake for 35 minutes or until a toothpick inserted in the center of each loaf comes out clean.

6. To freeze, wrap each loaf in plastic wrap and then foil.

Peace, Child . . . Peace

Maybe you've had it up to HERE today with kids
fighting, neighbors squabbling, or coworkers who
are just plain disagreeable. You're tired of it all and
wish you could order everyone to get along. But
your calls for peace in the midst of conflict go over
like a frog swimming in a punch bowl, and things
just get messier. The good news is that we don't run
the world—God does. We can't control how others
behave, but centered within each follower of Jesus is a
priceless gift: the Holy Spirit. Isaiah 26:3 tells us that
he'll keep in perfect peace all who trust in him and
whose thoughts are fixed on him. It's a promise.

[Jesus said,] "I am leaving you with a gift—peace
of mind and heart. And the peace I give is a gift the
world cannot give. So don't be troubled or afraid."
JOHN 14:27

God can take our broken pieces and give unbroken peace.
W. D. Gough

Keep your earrings
sorted and tidy in an
ice cube tray or mini
muffin tin.

TIP

Jump off the Bandwagon

If you "stand by your man" or swear allegiance to your alma mater or a certain political party, you could be considered loyal. Loyalty, that quality of being someone whom others can count on without question, is nearly always a wonderful characteristic—until it's not. Sometimes unquestioning loyalty can blind you to the faults of another person or institution until you're not even aware that you've lost your values or are setting a poor example for others. It's important to remain loyal to your ideals and the truth of God's Word, but be careful of blind allegiance to something or someone who no longer merits your trust.

They are all guilty of treason against Caesar, for they profess allegiance to another king, named Jesus.

ACTS 17:7

Discernment looks beneath the surface
and reads between the lines.

Charles Swindoll, Come Before Winter and Share My Hope

When Life Puts the Squeeze on You

Life is sweet, until it's not. Tough times come to us all. Sometimes they're of our own making. Did your mama ever tell you that if you lie down with dogs, you'll get up with fleas? Other times there's nothing you could've done to prevent the problems pestering you. Maybe while you were looking in one direction, a dump truck of trouble came barreling from another. We can't prevent a lot of the woes that come our way, but we can let go of our expectations for how we thought life would be. Thank God for his promise to supply all your needs, and trust him to make something good out of the mess. When life squeezes you like a lemon, just add some meringue—then you've got a pie!

I have learned how to be content with whatever I have. I know how to live on almost nothing or with everything. I have learned the secret of living in every situation, whether it is with a full stomach or empty, with plenty or little.
PHILIPPIANS 4:11-12

May you have the hindsight to know where you've been, the foresight to know where you're going, and the insight to know when you're going too far! *

* *Irish Blessings: A Photographic Celebration*

SHIRLEY'S CHOCOLATE ZUCCHINI BREAD

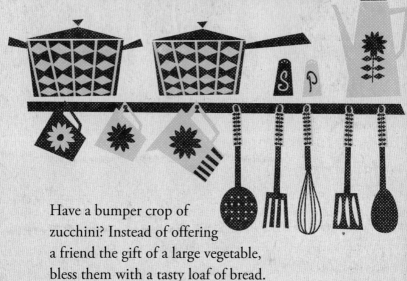

Have a bumper crop of zucchini? Instead of offering a friend the gift of a large vegetable, bless them with a tasty loaf of bread.

✻ INGREDIENTS

3 eggs
1 cup vegetable oil
2 cups granulated sugar
2 cups grated zucchini (about two small zucchini)
1 teaspoon vanilla extract

3 cups all-purpose flour
⅓ cup unsweetened baking cocoa
1 teaspoon salt
1 teaspoon baking soda
¼ teaspoon baking powder

✳ INSTRUCTIONS

1. Preheat oven to 350 degrees. Grease two 8½ x 4½ loaf pans.

2. In a large bowl, beat eggs until they become a light-yellow color; add oil and sugar, followed by zucchini and vanilla.

3. In a separate large bowl, sift together the flour, cocoa, salt, baking soda, and baking powder, and add to egg mixture. Mix until combined.

4. Pour batter into prepared loaf pans. Bake 45 minutes or until a toothpick inserted in the middle of each loaf comes out clean.

Have FOMO?

Some folks say that when a window of opportunity opens, you should never pull down the shade! Does that mean you need to say yes to everything someone asks you to try? FOMO sounds Southern for "four more," but it's actually short for "fear of missing out." If you've ever felt anxious because you thought you had missed out on something, you know how FOMO feels. Scripture tells us to make the most of every opportunity, but we also need to consider what it says just before and after that command. If we choose our activities carefully with thought beforehand, we can be confident we won't be full of regret afterward.

 Be careful how you live. Don't live like fools, but like those who are wise. Make the most of every opportunity in these evil days. Don't act thoughtlessly, but understand what the Lord wants you to do.
EPHESIANS 5:15-17

Find out who you are and do it on purpose.
Dolly Parton

Instead of using a
spoon to fill deviled
eggs, mash the cooked
yolks in a sealed
plastic baggie. Add
the other ingredients,
reseal, and knead
thoroughly. Cut off a
corner of the baggie
and squeeze the mixture
into the egg halves.
Easy cleanup!

TIP

Keep an Extinguisher Handy

Maybe you've heard that old warning about playing with fire. Even if you've been raised on sweet tea and Jesus, you know what it's like to be enticed to do what you shouldn't. We're fooling ourselves if we think we can get away with giving in to wrong behavior, such as taking something or even *someone* belonging to another. You might be able to hide the fire, but what're you gonna do with the smoke? Best not to start a blaze in the first place! When you're tempted to do something you know is wrong, talk to God about it. He's promised to keep the temptation from being too much for you and to point the way out of the situation.

Can a man scoop a flame into his lap
and not have his clothes catch on fire?
PROVERBS 6:27

The temptations in your life are no different from what others experience. And God is faithful. He will not allow the temptation to be more than you can stand. When you are tempted, he will show you a way out so that you can endure.
1 CORINTHIANS 10:13

Like a Hammock between Cornstalks

How many times have you heard someone say they want to live a "balanced" life—equal parts work, sleep, and family or personal time? Sure sounds good, but if you manage to do it all the time, you'll be the first person on earth to achieve it. It's a little like trying to sling a hammock between cornstalks—something's bound to fall! Attempting to line up in equal measure all the moving pieces of your life just doesn't work, but here's what does: granting yourself some spandex in your schedule. When your family needs you most, flex. When your job demands extra time, don't let anyone sell you a ticket for a guilt trip. And when you need to rest, take time for that too. That hammock has a purpose after all!

Seek [the LORD's] will in all you do,
and he will show you which path to take.
PROVERBS 3:6

What feels like the end of you may actually
just be the end of the old you.
Beth Moore, Entrusted

If you don't know
what to do for someone,
feed them.

HONEY-LET-ME-TELL-YA CAKE

Until recent times, residents of the Smoky Mountains traditionally depended on honey for food and trade, as well as a cash crop. This vintage recipe uses ingredients they had right on hand.

❋ INGREDIENTS

½ cup butter, softened
1 cup honey
1 egg, beaten well
2 cups all-purpose flour

1 teaspoon baking powder
½ teaspoon salt
½ teaspoon cinnamon
½ cup buttermilk

INSTRUCTIONS

1. Preheat oven to 350 degrees. Generously grease an 8-inch square pan.

2. Cream butter in a medium-sized bowl. Add honey and egg; mix to combine.

3. In a smaller bowl, sift together flour, baking powder, salt, and cinnamon.

4. Alternate adding buttermilk and dry mixture to creamed mixture. Mix well after each addition.

5. Pour batter into prepared pan and bake for 45 minutes or until a toothpick inserted in the center comes out clean.

Love Them Anyway

People come into our lives in all sorts of ways. Sometimes we choose our friends, neighbors, and coworkers, and other times they pick us. Occasionally we're stuck with each other whether we want to be or not. Maybe you work with someone who seems hell-bent on giving you a hard time, or you have a neighbor who's just plumb ornery. No matter how often you turn the other cheek, they're determined to slap it. Unhappy people often try to make other people unhappy too. It's said we meet people for a reason—they're either a blessin' or a lesson. If you can't find the blessin', take a lesson from Jesus, who taught us to love and pray for our enemies. It's the best road to meeting them someday as friends.

[Jesus said,] "You have heard the law that says, 'Love your neighbor' and hate your enemy. But I say, love your enemies! Pray for those who persecute you!"
MATTHEW 5:43-44

Love is not an inconvenience. It's a "get to," not a "have to."
Pastor Chris Westmoreland

To make a perfume's
fragrance last longer,
keep the bottle in its
original packaging
and store in a cool,
dry place out of
direct sunlight.

TIP

Don't Put It Off

None of us would willingly open our front door to someone we know will steal from us, but there's a sly robber we invite in practically every day—the thief of our time. When we know what we ought to be doing and we keep putting it off, we rob ourselves. It's easy to make excuses, rationalizing that we'll get to something right away or maybe in a little while. But you know what? "Right away" has already passed, and "a little while" can turn into a very long time. Make up your mind to do that hard thing first, knowing you'll feel such relief afterward. You'll never plow a field by just turning it over in your mind!

Don't just listen to God's word. You must do what it says. Otherwise, you are only fooling yourselves.

JAMES 1:22

No idleness, no laziness, no procrastination;
never put off till tomorrow what you can do today.
Johan De Witt

I've Got the Joy

If you grew up going to Sunday school, you might have enthusiastically belted out the old chorus about having "joy, joy, joy, joy" down in your heart—"to stay!" As you've gotten older, though, unbridled joy has become more elusive, hasn't it? Trying to capture it is like chasing the wind. Unless you can find the source, joy will escape your grasp every time. Maybe that's why Philippians 4:4 urges us, "Always be full of joy in the Lord. I say it again—rejoice!" When you look at that command closely, you'll see that it's telling us to return to the source of our joy, which is the peace and hope that come through a personal relationship with Jesus Christ. When you have the assurance of his steadfast love for you, you really do have joy down in your heart to stay!

Let all who take refuge in you rejoice;
let them sing joyful praises forever.

PSALM 5:11

Joy isn't waiting for some more convenient time.
It's present now, pushing through the noise of
your circumstances like a hungry teen at a potluck.

Cynthia Ruchti

On taking care
of babies: In one
end and out the other
makes a lot of work
for Mother.*

MISS EUNICE'S
HOT-FUDGE-IN-A-JAR

Store any leftovers in the fridge. When you need hot fudge topping, reheat for about 30 seconds in the microwave. This makes a great gift too!

✳ INGREDIENTS

1 cup light corn syrup
1 12-ounce package of semi-sweet chocolate chips
2 tablespoons butter

Quart-sized mason jar
½ cup whole milk
½ teaspoon vanilla extract

 # INSTRUCTIONS

1. Combine corn syrup, chocolate chips, and butter in the jar.

2. Microwave the jar (without the lid) on high for 2 minutes.
   Remove from the microwave carefully (the jar will be hot!) and
   stir the melted ingredients until smooth.

3. Blend in the milk and vanilla. A butter knife works great for this.

4. Serve hot fudge over ice cream. So good!

Honest to Goodness

Have you ever had to work a little too hard to tell the truth? Maybe you've spun a fanciful tale or two, or have stretched the truth till it's so out of shape even you can't recognize it. Or maybe little white lies have become a tad too big and convenient. If honesty is the best policy and you're not a trustworthy policyholder, take a close look at why expressing truth makes you uncomfortable. Deep inside, we all want to be known as someone who is reliable and whose word is never questioned. Plus there's a hidden benefit: When you're habitually honest, you don't have to worry about having a poor memory!

If you are faithful in little things, you will be faithful in large ones. But if you are dishonest in little things, you won't be honest with greater responsibilities.
LUKE 16:10

Don't assent to slander by staying silent.
Speak up and stand for the truth.
Maggie Wallem Rowe

Spinach and other greens stored in a plastic baggie will stay fresh even longer if you add a dry paper towel to soak up moisture.

TIP

R-E-S-P-E-C-T

When singer-songwriter Otis Redding released "Respect" in 1965 and Aretha Franklin recorded a variation of the song in 1967, neither artist could have predicted it would become one of the most memorable musical hits of the twentieth century. What is it about respect that we human beings crave so much? It's more than our desire to win others' approval or to be liked. You see, we can't demand respect. Respect is like cow's milk—you can't take it; it's got to be given. It's hard to win and easy to lose. If you long to be respected, live your life with integrity—keep your word, honor your commitments, and take responsibility for your actions. And remember: To get respect, you need to give it first.

There will be glory and honor and peace
from God for all who do good.
ROMANS 2:10

The power of servanthood. It commands respect.
It does not *demand* it.
Elisabeth Elliot, The Mark of a Man

Live Soul Strong

There's an old prayer that says, "Lord, either lighten my burden or strengthen my back." Truth be told, wouldn't we all rather have the former? When we add up our worries about our families, finances, and friends' situations, sometimes it's all just *too much*. Life's full of problems, and if we don't have enough, others will happily give us theirs. We can work out or lift weights or do whatever we can to build muscle, but the stressors of life on planet Earth have a way of bringing each of us to our knees. And maybe that's just where we need to be—on our knees before the only One who can give us the strength of soul equal to the demands of our days. No matter how you're feeling physically today, you can live soul strong!

March on, my soul; be strong!

JUDGES 5:21, NIV

Our spiritual journey is . . . not just a matter of physical perseverance or even mental determination. It's a deep commitment and an even deeper empowerment. I call it *soul strong.*

Lucinda Secrest McDowell, Soul Strong

If [God] has led you to this Red Sea of yours, he'll bring you through it somehow. *

*Archibald Alexander, The Glory in the Grey

84

IF-LIFE-GIVES-YOU-LEMONS PIE

This sweet treat is often called "icebox pie," but it will be gone so fast you won't have any leftovers to put in the fridge!

✳ INGREDIENTS

16 ounces cream cheese (two 8-ounce packages), softened
1 can (14 ounces) sweetened condensed milk

Juice of two lemons and grated zest from one
1 prepared graham cracker piecrust

 # INSTRUCTIONS

1. Beat softened cream cheese in mixing bowl with electric mixer.

2. Add sweetened condensed milk, lemon juice, and lemon zest; mix well.

3. Pour into piecrust and refrigerate two hours before digging in. For a special touch, serve with raspberry sauce or a dollop of whipped cream.

Pretty Is as Pretty Does

We all like receiving compliments about our appearance, don't we? When it's a good hair day or you're wearing a favorite outfit, it's gratifying when others notice. And when someone describes you as good-looking, it's natural to feel a little flattered. That's all fine and dandy . . . to a point. But remember the old saying that it's what's inside that counts? You might be the finest-looking person in the county, but if you are unkind or act ugly toward others, it won't matter. What people will remember is how poorly you made them feel. No matter how nicely a package is wrapped, it's not the paper and bow that make it valuable. Pretty is as pretty does!

The LORD doesn't see things the way you
see them. People judge by outward appearance,
but the LORD looks at the heart.

1 SAMUEL 16:7

Before you garden
without gloves, run
your fingernails
across a bar of soap.
Now you have a barrier
to prevent dirt from
getting under your
nails. Use a nailbrush
when you wash up
afterward.

TIP

Just Wait till I Tell Your Father

If your daddy was the disciplinarian in your house when you were growing up, you probably dreaded it when, after you had disobeyed, your mother threatened, "Just wait till your father gets home!" Maybe it was a small infraction, but the thought of the correction to come cast a big shadow over your mind. Sometimes the fear of punishment can be worse than the punishment itself. Our heavenly Father disciplines his children, too, but we never need to fear his hand. Sometimes he permits us to experience the consequences of our own willful choices, while other times he uses tough times to teach us lessons we can only learn the hard way. But at all times he loves us!

Think about it: Just as a parent disciplines a child, the LORD your God disciplines you for your own good.
DEUTERONOMY 8:5

The Beauty of Community

If you've ever lived in a rural area, you might have witnessed what happens when livestock escape and trample an adjacent field or yard. Tensions run high when property damage is involved. No wonder Robert Frost observed that good fences make good neighbors! But to take it a step further, good neighbors also make sure there's a gate in that fence, one that swings wide to welcome a stranger in need. That stranger might just one day be the one you need as well. When God said it's not good for man to be alone, he wasn't referring only to marriage. When we are willing to come alongside those nearby in love and service, we're doing just what God has commanded. That statement Jesus made about loving your neighbor? He meant it!

Love your neighbor as yourself.
MATTHEW 22:39

No one is rich enough to do without a neighbor.
Danish proverb

Expectations are premeditated offenses. People do what they do for their own reasons, and it rarely has anything to do with you!

*PeggySue Wells

SWEETIE-POTATO PIE

Similar to pumpkin pie but fluffier. And you don't need a holiday reason to fix it.

✳ INGREDIENTS

1 prepared piecrust
3 eggs
2¼ cups cooked, mashed sweet potatoes (4–5 medium)
½ cup brown sugar
1 teaspoon cinnamon

¼ teaspoon ground nutmeg
¼ teaspoon ground cloves
1⅓ cups whole milk
½ tablespoon butter, melted
Dash of salt

 **INSTRUCTIONS**

1. Preheat oven to 400 degrees. Line a 9-inch pie plate with piecrust.

2. Beat eggs in a large bowl until frothy.

3. Add mashed sweet potatoes, sugar, spices, milk, butter, and salt, mixing until smooth. Pour filling into the crust.

4. Bake for 20 minutes; then lower oven temperature to 375 degrees and bake another 15–20 minutes until almost set. (Filling should be a little jiggly in the center, but a toothpick inserted 1 inch from the edge should come out clean.)

5. Cool on a wire rack before slicing. Serve at room temperature.

God Will Provide

In a time not long past, a father might have looked at a young man courting his daughter with an eye to whether the suitor would be a "good provider." These days, most women—as well as men, thank you kindly—have ample opportunities to provide for themselves. But hard times are common to us all, aren't they? A drought can wipe out the crops, or a recession can drain our bank accounts drier than the Israelites' path through the Red Sea. Remember the gospel story of the little boy with the loaves and the fishes? There was only enough to feed a lad. But when those provisions were placed into the hands of Jesus, they multiplied to feed a multitude. Never under-estimate the depth of God's love—or the size of his storehouse—when it comes to your personal needs.

All humanity finds shelter in the shadow of your wings!
You feed them from the abundance of your own house,
letting them drink from your river of delights.
PSALM 36:7-8

God will always provide. It just might look different
from what we had in mind.
Maggie Wallem Rowe

Bothered by fruit flies?
Pour a few ounces of
vinegar over a piece of
overripe fruit in a jar.
Make a cone out of a piece
of paper and stick it in
the jar, narrow end down.
The mixture will attract
the flies, but they won't
be able to crawl back out
of the cone.

Patience, Sweet Pea . . . Patience

✳

If your parents didn't have much time for you when you were little, maybe you were still blessed to have a grandparent or an older person in your life who gave you their attention, no matter how tired they were. They never seemed to run out of patience. Now that you're older, you marvel at the perseverance they had putting up with you! How do some people learn to be so tolerant, managing children or challenging circumstances without complaint, while others get their feathers ruffled at the smallest difficulty? Patience is the ability to take the long view even when life hands you the short end of the stick. It doesn't come naturally to little ones, but it sure is handy for big people. It reins us in when we're tempted to lash out and zips our lips when we want to speak before we think. Ask God to help you learn to bide your time.

Rejoice in our confident hope. Be patient in trouble,
and keep on praying.
ROMANS 12:12

You're the Genuine Article

Have you ever been called "The real McCoy"? Whatever the source of that phrase, it's a compliment when others know you're genuine to your core. Whether they like you or not, they know who they're dealing with, and that earns respect. To be truly authentic is to be exactly who you claim to be—the same on the inside as you appear on the outside. Wouldn't it be wonderful if everyone we met was that trustworthy? When you live as your authentic self, you've got no competition. Rhinestones are perfectly fine as long as they don't pretend to be diamonds!

Jesus said, "Now here is a genuine son of Israel—
a man of complete integrity."
JOHN 1:47

Authenticity is a collection of choices that we have to make every day. It's about the choice to show up and be real. The choice to be honest. The choice to let our true selves be seen.
Brené Brown, The Gifts of Imperfection

Save energy: When not in use, turn off the juice!*

*US Department of Energy's 2005 theme

SUNDAY FRIED CHICKEN

Don't skip the buttermilk
soak—it's the secret to
perfect Southern fried chicken. In my opinion,
the results are even better than the Colonel's!

✳ INGREDIENTS

1 whole cut-up chicken
1 teaspoon salt
1 teaspoon pepper
2 cups buttermilk

Self-rising flour for dredging
Vegetable or canola oil for
   frying
Deep-fry thermometer

✳ INSTRUCTIONS

1. Season chicken with salt and pepper and place in a shallow dish.

2. Pour buttermilk over chicken and cover with foil or plastic wrap. Refrigerate two hours or more.

3. Discard the buttermilk and dredge chicken pieces in flour.

4. In either a Dutch oven or deep skillet, heat 2 inches of oil to 360 degrees. Add chicken pieces a few at a time (don't crowd). Cover with lid and fry 6 minutes.

5. Uncover the chicken and cook an additional 9 minutes. Use tongs to turn the chicken; cover and fry 6 more minutes. Uncover again and cook 7–9 minutes, turning pieces for even browning. Drain chicken on paper towels. Repeat the process for each batch of pieces, until all the chicken is fried.

For the Love of God

Have you ever felt forced to work like a one-armed paperhanger to earn someone else's love and approval? Maybe you struggled with a parent who was hard to please or a teacher who was seldom satisfied with your efforts. Could be you were sweet on someone who never made you feel "good enough." Yet that's not the way it is with God and his children. His love is unconditional—there's nothing we need to do to earn it. In fact, Scripture tells us God's kindness and love are what save us, not anything we've done. If we had to work for his favor, we'd be tempted to brag about our efforts. As it is, he loves us without exception and without restriction. No fine print! When it comes to the love of God, aren't you amazed by his grace?

When God our Savior revealed his kindness and love, he saved us, not because of the righteous things we had done, but because of his mercy. He washed away our sins, giving us a new birth and new life through the Holy Spirit.

TITUS 3:4-5

Clean tarnished silverware with water you've boiled potatoes in. After you've removed the potatoes, turn off the burner, drop your silverware in the pan, swish, and let sit for an hour. Remove and wash. Voilà!

Everyone Can Help Someone

❋

Have you ever witnessed someone responding to another person's need by offering sympathy or promising to pray, yet they still don't step up to help in practical ways? Some people are about as handy as a back pocket on a shirt, while others quietly make themselves useful in countless ways. It's easy to say we care, but if we want to actually *show* we do, we need to put our muscles where our mouths are. Do you know a certain individual who needs a ride to the doctor or a family who needs a meal? Can you muster folks from your church, neighborhood, or community to come alongside those who lack resources? Matthew 25:40 tells us that when we serve "the least of these"—those who lack power or are often overlooked—we are serving Christ himself.

Share each other's burdens, and in this way
obey the law of Christ.
GALATIANS 6:2

Being useful is more important than being noticed.
Gail MacDonald

On the One Hand . . .

You've got a big decision to make, but you keep tossing your options back and forth like flapjacks flipped by a short-order cook. On the one hand, the situation might turn out just as you are hoping. On the other hand, you're scared to think about what might happen if you guess wrong. You need a third hand! You could seek advice, but picking the wrong person might be like asking a barber whether you need a haircut. Where do you get the wisdom to choose the right thing? Scripture tells us that all we need to do is ask God. Our heavenly Father delights in stepping in when his children come to him for help. Spend time in his Word, listen hard, and trust his Spirit to lead you. He cares about the outcome even more than you do.

If you need wisdom, ask our generous God, and he will give it to you.
JAMES 1:5

Wisdom comes with age, but sometimes age comes alone!
Anonymous

The older the fiddle, the sweeter the tune.*

*Irish proverb

COUNTRY BEAN SALAD

There is just enough
sweetness to make this the
tastiest healthy salad you've ever had.
Try it with scoop-style tortilla chips.

✳ INGREDIENTS

Beans and Vegetables

1 15-ounce can pinto beans
1 15-ounce can black beans
1 15-ounce can corn
1 medium onion, diced

1 cup chopped celery
1 cup chopped red or green
  bell pepper

Dressing

- ¼ cup vegetable or canola oil
- ¼ cup white vinegar
- ⅓ cup granulated sugar
- ½ teaspoon salt
- ¼ teaspoon pepper

 INSTRUCTIONS

1. Drain and rinse pinto beans, black beans, and corn.

2. Combine pinto beans, black beans, corn, onion, celery, and peppers.

3. Combine the dressing ingredients in a small pan and heat until the sugar is melted. Cool dressing at least one hour before pouring over bean mixture. Refrigerate until chilled. Consume within three days.

Attitude Is a Choice

The next time you have a glass of lemonade or sweet tea handy, take a quick look: Is it half-full or half-empty? Folks will say you can tell an optimist from a pessimist by how they view that glass. But here's another way to consider the matter: You are mighty fortunate to have a glass at all! UCLA basketball coach John Wooden was known for saying that things turn out best for people who make the best of how things turn out. Sometimes we're afraid to hope that good things will happen for fear of being disappointed, but God never intended his children to live in fear. You can't choose your circumstances, but as sure as the sun comes up in the morning, you can choose how you look at them!

For the despondent, every day brings trouble;
for the happy heart, life is a continual feast.
PROVERBS 15:15

Think of the Beatitudes that Jesus taught as the *be*-attitudes:
Be humble. Be thankful. Be merciful.
Maggie Wallem Rowe

Use unflavored
dental floss—
before you've used
it on your teeth!—
to cleanly cut
slices of cake.

TIP

God with Us

❋

Carter, a little boy in North Carolina, loved to share his bed with his dog. One night after the pet had been outside, Carter's parents insisted the dog was just too dirty and had to sleep in his crate instead. The next morning, they were startled to find their young son fast asleep in the kennel, curled up next to his beloved friend. Does this true story bring a truth from the Bible to mind? Scripture teaches us that God loves us so much that he sent his only Son into the world to live in our midst. The fact that we were filthy from sin didn't stop Jesus from making his home with us. That's the meaning of the name *Immanuel*: God with us!

I know the LORD is always with me. I will not be shaken, for he is right beside me.

PSALM 16:8

Look! The virgin will conceive a child! She will give birth to a son, and they will call him Immanuel, which means "God is with us."

MATTHEW 1:23

You Can Do It!

Ever had a challenge so tough it felt like stuffing a feather pillow in a windstorm or setting a picnic table in a hurricane? Or maybe you've been so short of money you had to fry up your nest egg! Life's full of problems and perplexities, but those situations also make us strong. An African proverb says that smooth seas do not make skillful sailors. Instead of limiting the challenges in your life, try to challenge your limits. When we persevere through tough times, seeing them as opportunities for growth, we not only stretch our own capabilities but also inspire others to do the same. Take this as your personal pledge today: "With God's help, I can do this!"

Our God . . . we do not know what to do, but our eyes are on you.
2 CHRONICLES 20:12, ESV

As aerodynamic engineers "proved" many years ago, *the bumblebee cannot fly!* Its wings are too weak and its body is too heavy. Fortunately the bumblebee doesn't know that and goes right on flying.
Mary Kay Ash, Mary Kay on People Management

Don't judge people too quickly. You can't tell the size of turnips by lookin' at their tops.

SWEETLY SOUTHERN TEA

Sweet tea is a favorite beverage in many parts of the world, but in the South it's an art form! Here's a classic recipe to enjoy on your front porch.

 INGREDIENTS

Simple Syrup

1 cup water

1 cup granulated sugar

Tea

12 tea bags

1 quart (4 cups) ice cubes

⅛ teaspoon baking soda

1¼ cups simple syrup

1 quart (4 cups) fresh water

 # INSTRUCTIONS

Simple Syrup

1. In a small saucepan, bring water and sugar to a boil over medium-high heat, stirring frequently. Boil 1 minute or until sugar dissolves.

2. Remove from heat and cool 30 minutes. Unused syrup can be refrigerated in a closed container up to two weeks.

Tea

1. Place tea bags and baking soda in a 2-quart heatproof glass pitcher.

2. Bring water just to a rolling boil in a pan or kettle and immediately pour over tea bags, keeping them submerged.

3. Cover pitcher and steep tea bags for 7 minutes. Remove and discard bags. Add ice to pitcher and stir tea until ice melts.

4. Stir in 1¼ cups simple syrup and serve tea over ice. *Aah . . .*

Say You're Sorry

We likely all remember times when we misbehaved as kids and our parents had to force us to apologize. Admitting fault doesn't get any easier when we grow older. Whether we call it pride or stubbornness or just being plain pigheaded, it's hard to fess up when we're at fault. Sometimes we stall or drag our feet for so long that the opportunity passes and the relationship is permanently damaged. Maybe the other person was responsible, too, but someone needs to be strong enough to step forward and ask forgiveness to set things right. The best way to eat crow is while it's still warm, 'cause the colder it gets, the harder it is to swallow!

Do all that you can to live in peace with everyone.
ROMANS 12:18

Be kind to each other, tenderhearted, forgiving one another, just as God through Christ has forgiven you.
EPHESIANS 4:32

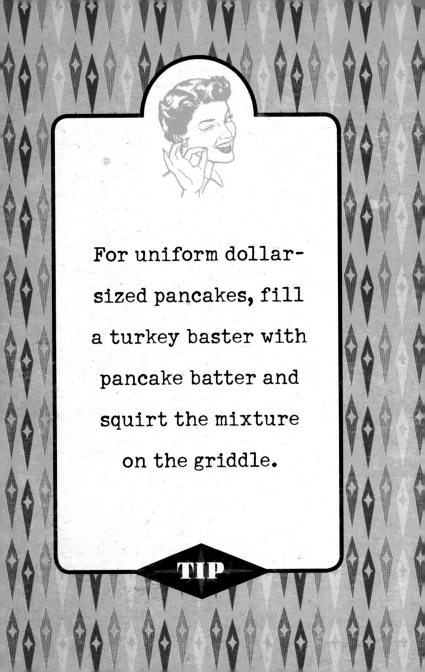

For uniform dollar-
sized pancakes, fill
a turkey baster with
pancake batter and
squirt the mixture
on the griddle.

TIP

Holier than Thou?

Have you ever been pressured to do something you were uncomfortable with, only to be accused of being "holier than thou" when you refused? If you convey an attitude of being sanctimonious or morally superior to another person, maybe the label fits. But what if you're truly trying to follow the commandments of Christ, living in a way that pleases him and protects others and yourself? Holiness is nothing more or less than knowing you've been set apart by God to fulfill the special purpose that he has for your life's journey here on earth. Striving to be holy isn't trying to be better than other people—it's becoming more like Jesus.

Even before he made the world, God loved us and chose us in Christ to be holy and without fault in his eyes.
EPHESIANS 1:4

Holiness means something more than the sweeping away of the old leaves of sin: it means the life of Jesus developed in us.
Lilias Trotter, Parables of the Cross

A Heart as Soft as Butter

Some people have hearts as soft as summer butter, while the hearts of certain others are hard as last week's cornbread. What causes one person to feel tender sympathy for the needs in their neighborhood or around the world when another seems to care only for herself? If you are blessed with young ones in your life, you know how important it is to teach them to have compassion for those who lack what so many take for granted, like food, shelter, and access to clean water. Your children will learn best by helping you actually do something tangible to meet others' needs. Just as God has shown mercy to us, we need to open our hearts, hands, and wallets to help those around us.

[Jesus said,] "You must be compassionate, just as your Father is compassionate."
LUKE 6:36

There is nothing more ugly than a Christian orthodoxy without understanding or without compassion.
Francis A. Schaeffer, The God Who Is There

Joy is sorrow inside out.*

*Hannah Hunard, *Mountains of Spices*

Security and Exchange

Maybe you've seen those products that calm a pet's anxiety during storms—a weighted vest, pressure wrap, or shirt that simulates a protective hug. When life is stressful and we're wound up tighter than a twenty-dollar watch, wouldn't it be nice to have a garment we could slip on that would instantly settle our nerves? It's natural to want security in our lives, to desire to be free from fear and worry. Just as we comfort our young ones, we long for someone to tell us that everything's gonna be okay. The good news is that God cares about every single detail of our lives, from our families to our jobs to those stacks of unpaid bills. We'll never be fully secure in this world, but we can exchange our fears for God's promise of eternal security in the next. And that's a promise you can take to the bank.

Jesus replied . . . "I give them eternal life, and they will never perish. No one can snatch them away from me, for my Father has given them to me, and he is more powerful than anyone else."

JOHN 10:25, 28-29

Confidence Looks Good on You, Girl!

❄

Do you ever feel like everyone else seems to have it together while your life is coming apart? Maybe you feel insecure about your appearance, your speech, or the upkeep of your home, and you can't help but envy those people who seem so self-assured. Would it help to know that almost all of us lack confidence when we compare our possessions with what others have or our appearance with how someone else looks? That's the culprit right there—comparison! God created each of us, and there is only *one* of us. Nobody can be *you* as well as you can. True confidence comes when we know we are uniquely loved by God just as we are.

I am confident I will see the LORD's goodness
while I am here in the land of the living.
PSALM 27:13

Through all the tears and fears I had to face,
I supplied the grit, and God supplied the grace.
Balsam Range, "Grit and Grace"

Birthdays are good for you. Statistics show that the people who have the most live the longest.*

*Larry Lorenzoni

The Best Way to Have a Friend

We never outgrow our need for friends. Some of your oldest friends may no longer be your closest friends, but the history you share will always be special. Some friendships, lost for a time, might return to you someday. And new friends may come into your life in wonderful ways you never expected. But here's the thing: It helps to think of friendship as a verb, not a noun. It's not something you have, but something you *do* by holding out an encouraging hand of support and affection when you can. Remember what your mama always said: "The best way to have a friend? Be one."

A friend loves at all times.
PROVERBS 17:17, ESV

Yes'm, old friends is always best, 'less you can catch a new one that's fit to make an old one out of.
Mrs. Todd in Sarah Orne Jewett's Country of the Pointed Firs

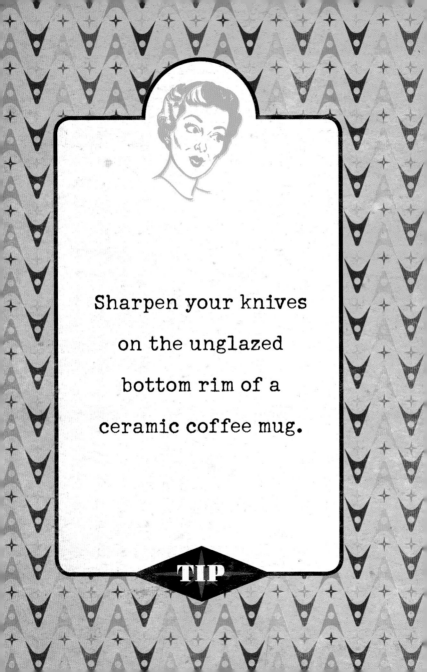

Sharpen your knives

on the unglazed

bottom rim of a

ceramic coffee mug.

TIP

Earth is forgiveness school.*

Goodness Gracious!

*G*race is such a lovely word. You see it on birth records, church signs, and plaques in gift shops. But what does it mean exactly? Bible scholars tell us that grace is God's unmerited favor, meaning that it's God's gift to us—nothing we earn by our own efforts. When you accept the gift of salvation through faith in Jesus Christ, that's pure grace. And when you extend mercy and forgiveness to someone who has hurt you, that's grace too. Grace has nothing to do with getting what we deserve, but everything to do with receiving what we do not. Goodness gracious, how amazing is grace!

God saved you by his grace when you believed.
And you can't take credit for this; it is a gift from God.
EPHESIANS 2:8

Grace means there is nothing I can do to make God love me more, and nothing I can do to make God love me less.
Philip Yancey, What's So Amazing about Grace?

If you crack an egg into
a bowl and notice a
tiny piece of eggshell
floating in the egg
white, scoop it up
with half of the shell
instead of a spoon. It's
a lot easier!

TIP

Beware of offering answers before you know what the questions are.

Outlive Your Life

✳

"**Y**ou're not the boss of me!" Maybe someone has thrown those exact words in your face. It could have been a child who refused to accept your authority or a coworker who was slacking off on the job. Could be that leadership isn't a comfortable fit on you, but you're in charge of this family or that committee, and the responsibility's all yours. Or is it? Our heavenly Father has given each of us what we need to fulfill our commitments. If God has asked you to take on a leadership role, he'll equip you with the skills. After all, those responsibilities are our response to *his* ability. Love your life as you live and lead well. Life is sweet, y'all!

 In his grace, God has given us different gifts for doing certain things well. . . . If God has given you leadership ability, take the responsibility seriously.

ROMANS 12:6, 8

Leadership is about making others better as a result of your presence and making sure that impact lasts in your absence.

Sheryl Sandberg

Also by Maggie Wallem Rowe

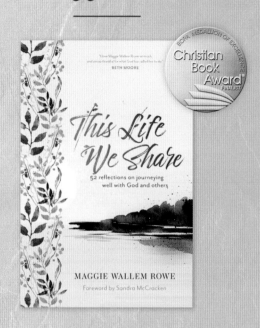

"How Maggie Wallem Rowe so nicely, and we are thankful for what God has called her to be."
BETH MOORE

This Life We Share

52 reflections on journeying
well with God and others

MAGGIE WALLEM ROWE

Foreword by Sandra McCracken

Forge fresh soul connections with your traveling companions and the God whose presence is infused in every moment of your journey. Consider *This Life We Share* your walking stick, water bottle, and warm companionship to help guide and refresh you on your journey. Enjoy reading and rereading these fifty-two reflections for timeless wisdom and practical principles that will inspire every season of your life.

Maggie Wallem Rowe is a writer and dramatist who lives in western North Carolina. Mama to three and grandma to six, Maggie loves mountain dancing, bluegrass, and barbecue.

CP1744